W9-AQI-466

First Biographies

John F. Kennedy

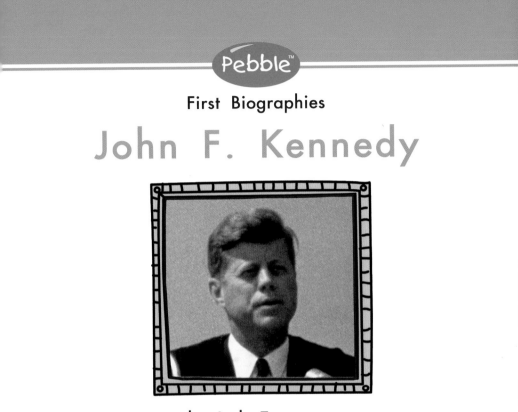

by Judy Emerson

Consulting Editor: Gail Saunders-Smith, Ph.D.
Consultant: James N. Druckman, Ph.D.
Assistant Professor of Political Science
University of Minnesota

Capstone
press
Mankato, Minnesota

Pebble Books are published by Capstone Press
151 Good Counsel Drive, P.O. Box 669, Mankato, Minnesota 56002
www.capstonepress.com

1 2 3 4 5 6 09 08 07 06 05 04

Library of Congress Cataloging-in-Publication Data
Emerson, Judy.
    John F. Kennedy / by Judy Emerson.
    p. cm.—(First biographies)
    Summary: A simple biography of the naval hero, congressman, and
president who was assassinated in 1963.
    Includes bibliographical references and index.
    ISBN 0-7368-2368-9 (hardcover)
    1. Kennedy, John F. (John Fitzgerald), 1917–1963—Juvenile literature.
2. Presidents—United States—Biography—Juvenile literature. [1. Kennedy, John F.
(John Fitzgerald), 1917–1963. 2. Presidents.] I. Title. II. Series: First biographies
(Mankato, Minn.)
E842.Z9E44 2004
973.922′092—dc22   2003015686

Note to Parents and Teachers

The First Biographies series supports national history standards
for units on people and culture. This book describes and illustrates
the life of John F. Kennedy. The photographs support early readers
in understanding the text. This book also introduces early readers
to subject-specific vocabulary words, which are defined in the
Glossary. Early readers may need assistance to read some words
and to use the Table of Contents, Glossary, Read More, Internet
Sites, and Index/Word List sections of the book.

Table of Contents

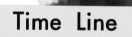

Time Line

1917
born

John F. Kennedy

John Fitzgerald Kennedy was born in Massachusetts in 1917. He had eight brothers and sisters.

◄ John with seven of his brothers and sisters

Time Line

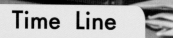

1917
born

1940
graduates
from Harvard

John was a good student. After high school, he studied history and politics at Harvard University.

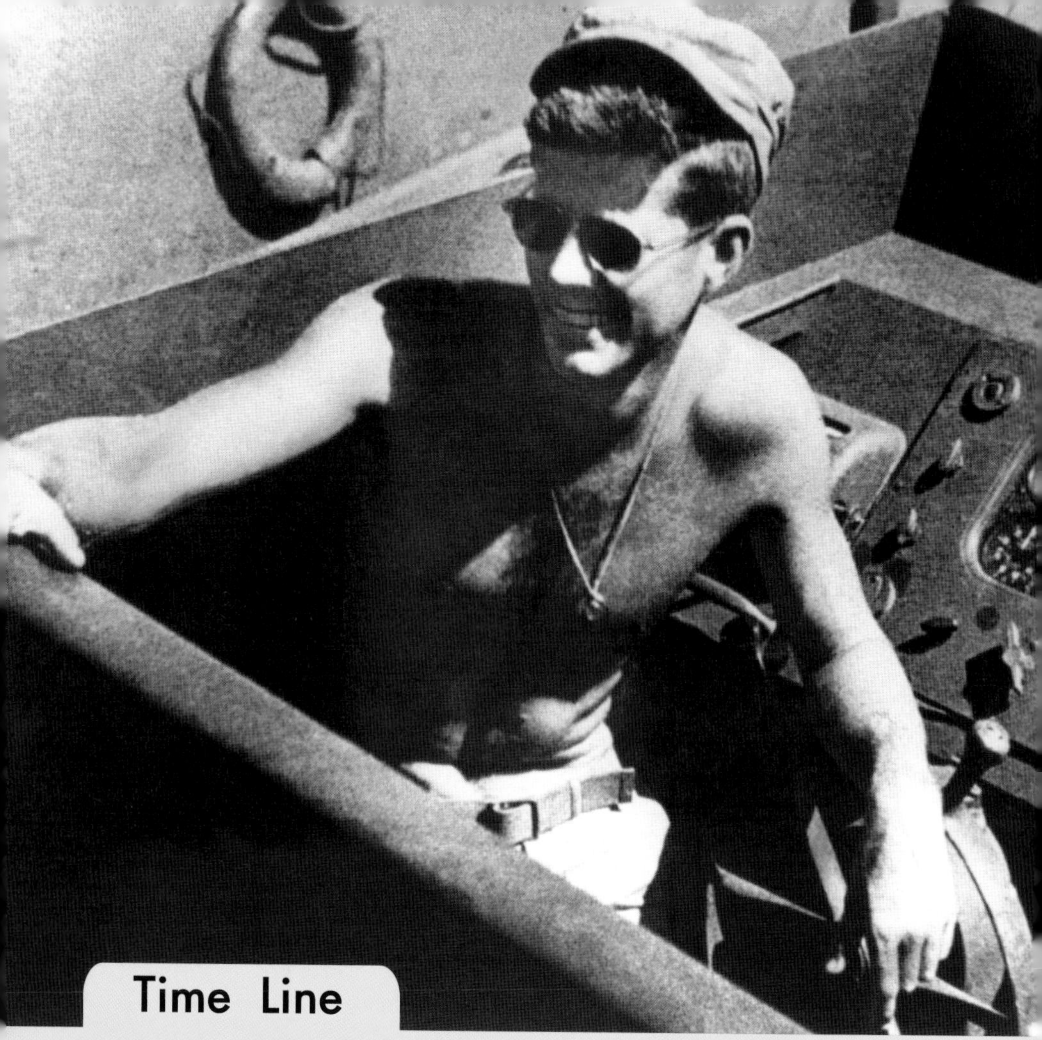

Time Line

1917
born

1940
graduates
from Harvard

1943
saves boat
crew members

During World War II, John was the leader of a boat crew in the U.S. Navy. The boat sank. John saved the lives of some crew members. People called him a hero.

John as leader of a U.S. Navy boat in 1943

Time Line

1917
born

1940
graduates
from Harvard

1943
saves boat
crew members

1952
elected to
Congress

John became a politician.
He was elected to the
U.S. Congress five times.
He worked hard to make
the United States better.

John as a senator from Massachusetts around 1953

Time Line

| 1917 born | 1940 graduates from Harvard | 1943 saves boat crew members | 1952 elected to Congress |

Marriage

In 1953, John married
Jacqueline Bouvier. She
was a newspaper reporter.
They had three children.
One child died as an infant.

◄ John and Jacqueline soon after getting married

1953
marries
Jacqueline Bouvier

Time Line

●	●	●	●
1917 born	1940 graduates from Harvard	1943 saves boat crew members	1952 elected to Congress

In 1956, John wrote
a book about leaders
and their ideas. Many
people read John's book.

◀ John signing copies of his book *Profiles in Courage*

1953
marries
Jacqueline Bouvier

Time Line

1917	1940	1943	1952
born	graduates from Harvard	saves boat crew members	elected to Congress

President Kennedy

In 1960, Americans elected John U.S. president. He was 43 years old. John's children sometimes played in his office.

John Jr. playing in John's office

1953
marries
Jacqueline Bouvier

1960
elected
president

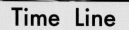

Time Line

●	●	●	●
1917 born	**1940** graduates from Harvard	**1943** saves boat crew members	**1952** elected to Congress

John was a busy president.
He worked for equal rights
and started the Peace Corps.
John worked to have
Americans explore space.

John working as president in 1961

1953
marries
Jacqueline Bouvier

1960
elected
president

ALL THE WAY WITH J.F.K.

Time Line

| 1917 born | 1940 graduates from Harvard | 1943 saves boat crew members | 1952 elected to Congress |

In 1963, John and his wife were riding in a parade in Dallas, Texas. John was shot and killed. People remember John F. Kennedy as a great president.

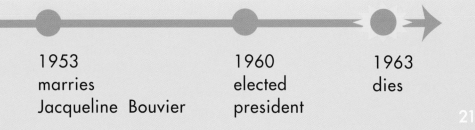

1953
marries
Jacqueline Bouvier

1960
elected
president

1963
dies

Glossary

Congress—the part of the government that makes laws

elect—to choose someone as a leader by voting; John was the youngest person elected president; he was 43 years old when he was elected.

explore—to discover what a place is like

hero—a person who shows strength and courage by doing a good thing for someone else

Peace Corps—an organization of trained volunteers from the United States that helps people in other countries; Peace Corps volunteers often help people with farming and education.

politician—someone who runs for or holds a government office

Read More

Franchino, Vicky. *John F. Kennedy.* Compass Point Early Biographies. Minneapolis: Compass Point Books, 2002.

Frost, Helen. *John F. Kennedy.* Famous Americans. Mankato, Minn.: Pebble Books, 2003.

Joseph, Paul. *John F. Kennedy.* United States Presidents. Edina, Minn.: Abdo Publishing, 2002.

Internet Sites

FactHound offers a safe, fun way to find Internet sites related to this book. All of the sites on FactHound have been researched by our staff.

Here's how:

1. Visit *www.facthound.com*
2. Type in this special code **0736823689** for age-appropriate sites. Or enter a search word related to this book for a more general search.
3. Click on the Fetch It button.

FactHound will fetch the best sites for you!

Index/Word List

Word Count: 191
Early-Intervention Level: 19

Editorial Credits

Mari C. Schuh, editor; Heather Kindseth, cover designer and illustrator; Enoch Peterson, production designer; Scott Thoms, photo researcher; Karen Risch, product planning editor

Photo Credits

Corbis/Bettmann, 20; Stanley Tretick 1963, 16
Getty Images/Hulton Archive, cover, 1, 6, 8, 10, 12, 18
JFK Library Foundation, 4
John F. Kennedy Library, 14